HAMMERHEAD SHARKS

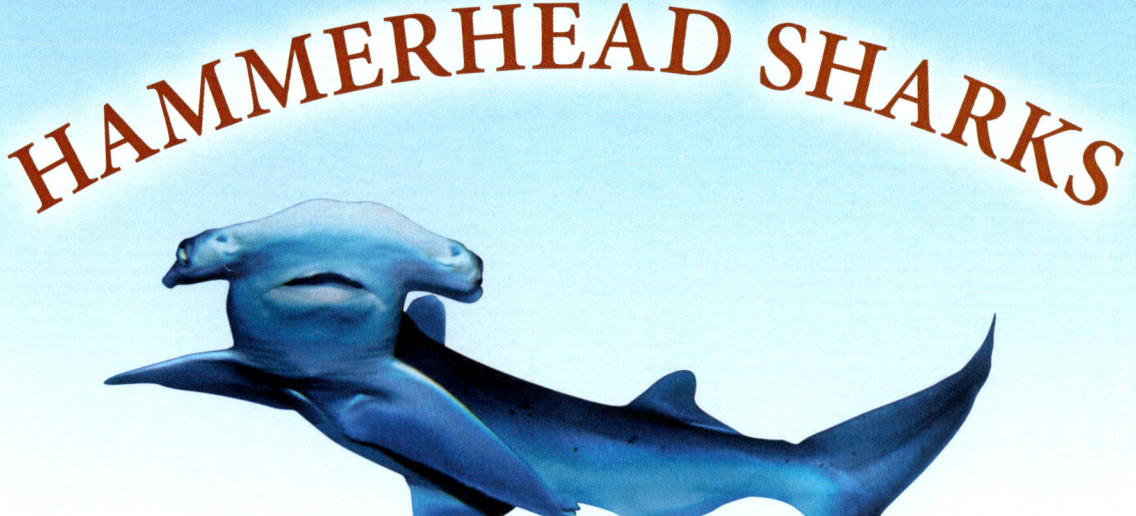

by Vicky Franchino

Children's Press®
An Imprint of Scholastic Inc.
New York Toronto London Auckland Sydney
Mexico City New Delhi Hong Kong
Danbury, Connecticut

Content Consultant
Dr. Stephen S. Ditchkoff
Professor of Wildlife Sciences
Auburn University
Auburn, Alabama

Photographs ©: age fotostock/Ron and Valerie Tay: cover; Alamy Images/Juniors Bildarchiv GmbH: 1, 12, 13, 46; Dreamstime/Vbotond: 2 background, 3 background, 44 background, 45 background; Getty Images: 26, 27 (Alexander Safonov), 4, 5 background, 22, 23 (Jonathan Bird), 7, 40 (Jones/Shimlock-Secret Sea Visions); Media Bakery: 30, 31 (Andre Seale), 14, 15 (E. Bradley), 10, 11 (Tom Brakefield); Oceanwidelmages.com: 5 top, 18, 19, 24, 25; Science Source: 39 (Frederick R. McConnaughey), 32, 33 (Millard H. Sharp); Shutterstock, Inc.: 28, 29 (Brandelet), 8, 9 (Shane Gross); Superstock, Inc.: 2, 3, 20, 21 (Flirt), 35 (Nicholas Eveleigh), 16, 17 (Steve Bloom Images), 5 bottom, 36.

Map by Bob Italiano

Library of Congress Cataloging-in-Publication Data
Franchino, Vicky.
 Hammerhead sharks / by Vicky Franchino.
    pages cm. — (Nature's children)
 Includes bibliographical references and index.
 Audience: Ages 9–12.
 Audience: Grades 4–6.
 ISBN 978-0-531-20668-3 (lib. bdg.) — ISBN 978-0-531-21661-3 (pbk.)
 1. Hammerhead sharks—Juvenile literature. I. Title.
 QL638.95.S7F73 2014
 597.3—dc23   2014001501

No part of this publication may be reproduced in whole or in part, or stored in a retrieval system, or transmitted in any form or by any means, electronic, mechanical, photocopying, recording, or otherwise, without written permission of the publisher. For information regarding permission, write to Scholastic Inc., Attention: Permissions Department, 557 Broadway, New York, NY 10012.
© 2015 Scholastic Inc.

All rights reserved. Published in 2015 by Children's Press, an imprint of Scholastic Inc.

Printed in China 62
SCHOLASTIC, CHILDREN'S PRESS, and associated logos are trademarks and/or registered trademarks of Scholastic Inc.

1 2 3 4 5 6 7 8 9 10 R 24 23 22 21 20 19 18 17 16 15

FACT FILE

Hammerhead Sharks

Class	Chondrichthyes
Order	Carcharhiniformes
Family	Sphyrnidae
Genera	Two genera
Species	10 species
World distribution	Found in tropical and temperate waters around the world
Habitat	Oceans, both shallow coastal areas and deepwater regions
Distinctive physical characteristics	Has a flat, wide head that resembles a hammer or shovel; one eye and one nostril located on the tip of each end of the head
Habits	Often travels in large groups called schools during the day and hunts alone at night; appears to swim almost continuously
Diet	Fish, squid, octopuses, crustaceans, and other sharks; stingrays are a favorite food

HAMMERHEAD SHARKS

Contents

CHAPTER 1
6 Ocean Dwellers

CHAPTER 2
14 A Helpful Head

CHAPTER 3
26 Social Life

CHAPTER 4
33 Family Ties

CHAPTER 5
38 Hard Times for Hammerheads

42 Words to Know
44 Habitat Map
46 Find Out More
47 Index
48 About the Author

CHAPTER 1

Ocean Dwellers

In the deep, dark waters of the ocean, a group of sharks swims in wide circles around an underwater mountain. There are sharks as far as the eye can see, hundreds and hundreds of them. They seem to move constantly, never stopping to rest. These are no ordinary sharks. Their heads are long and flat, with a wide staring eye on each side. They are hammerhead sharks. Viewed from below, the sharks are dark shadows moving through light blue water. Their bodies are long and sleek, with fins that push them easily through the sea.

The group begins to split up as day turns to night. It is time to hunt for dinner, and hammerheads like to eat alone. One hammerhead glides along the bottom of the ocean, hoping to find a stingray buried in the sand.

A group of scalloped hammerheads can include as many as 500 sharks.

One Big Fish

Sharks are a type of fish. Like most fish, they are cold-blooded. This means that a hammerhead's body temperature is the same as the temperature of its environment. Hammerhead sharks live in many oceans and seas around the world. They like water temperatures that are warm or mild. This keeps their body temperature from dropping too low. Some hammerheads live in shallow waters near the coast. Others can be found in deep water far from land.

    Hammerheads are usually grayish brown with a white belly. This helps them blend in with their surroundings. When the sharks are viewed from below, their light bellies are hard to see because of the sun shining down above the surface. When they're viewed from above, the sharks' coloring helps them blend in with the dark color of the ocean.

    The hammerhead shark's body is covered with denticles. These are tough, bony scales that protect the shark and help it move smoothly through the water.

Blending in with their surroundings helps hammerheads launch surprise attacks when they are hunting.

Ten Species

There are 10 species of hammerhead sharks. The largest is the great hammerhead. It can be up to 20 feet (6 meters) long and weigh up to 1,000 pounds (454 kilograms). The smallest is the scalloped bonnethead. It is about 35 inches (89 centimeters) long and weighs about 20 pounds (9 kg). Female hammerheads are usually larger and heavier than male hammerheads. The other hammerhead species are the scalloped hammerhead, the scoophead, the smalleye hammerhead, the bonnethead, the smooth hammerhead, the whitefin hammerhead, and the winghead. In late 2013, researchers discovered the tenth species: the Carolina hammerhead. It is very similar to the scalloped hammerhead.

Hammerheads are carnivores, which means that they eat animals. Fish, squid, crabs, octopuses, stingrays, and even small sharks are all part of their diet. Stingrays have painful stingers that help protect them from most predators. However, these defenses don't stop the hammerhead from enjoying its favorite meal.

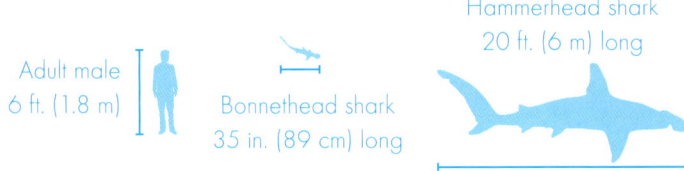

A bonnethead shark swims above the sand off the coast of the Bahamas.

No Bones About It

Hammerhead sharks have a skeleton that is made of cartilage, not bone. The human nose and ears are also made of cartilage. Cartilage is tough but flexible. It helps the hammerhead shark bend and flex as it travels through the water. Cartilage makes it easy for sharks to turn quickly as they swim. Scientists can usually look at an animal's bones to learn how old it is. Because hammerhead sharks don't have any bones, it can be very hard to know their age.

The hammerhead's fins are made of cartilage, too. The fins on the top of its body are called dorsal fins. They keep the shark from tipping over in the water. The fins on the hammerhead's belly are called pectoral fins. These fins help the shark turn and steer. The fin at the very back of the hammerhead shark's body is known as the caudal fin. This fin helps push the shark through the water.

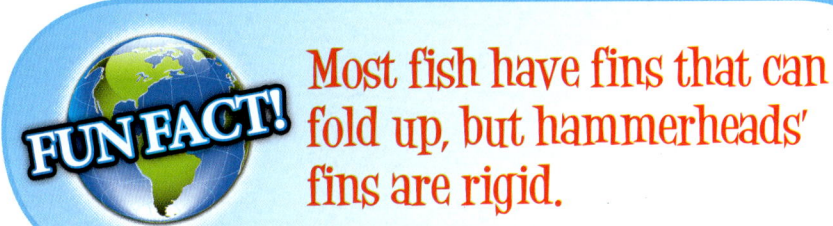

FUN FACT! Most fish have fins that can fold up, but hammerheads' fins are rigid.

A hammerhead's flexible skeleton helps make it an agile and effective hunter.

CHAPTER 2

A Helpful Head

The hammerhead gets its name from its unusually shaped head. Scientists call the shape at the end of a hammerhead's head a cephalofoil. The cephalofoil of each hammerhead species is slightly different. Some have a straight edge. Others are rounded. Many have notches. The bonnethead has a cephalofoil that is shaped like a shovel.

    The hammerhead's head shape gives the shark special abilities. One is excellent vision. The hammerhead has one eye on each end of its cephalofoil. This eye arrangement makes the hammerhead very good at judging how far away something is. Hammerheads can also see above and below them at all times, and they can see what's behind them with just a twist of the head. Good vision helps protect the hammerhead. If a larger shark is looking for dinner, the hammerhead has a good chance of seeing the predator first and making an escape.

Each species of hammerhead has a head shape that's suited to its particular habitat.

14

Smells and Sounds

The hammerhead shark has a very good sense of smell. It can notice a single drop of blood in the water, even from very far away. There is one nostril on each end of the hammerhead's cephalofoil. Because the nostrils are so spread out, they allow the hammerhead to smell a bigger area of the ocean at one time. This spacing also helps the shark determine what direction a smell is coming from. The hammerhead uses this sense to help it find food. There's one thing that the hammerhead doesn't use its nose for: breathing. Sharks breathe through their gills instead of their nostrils.

This shark's hearing is excellent, too. In the right conditions, a hammerhead can hear prey that is hundreds of feet away. The hammerhead listens carefully for the sound of a wounded animal, then goes in search of a meal.

 Although scientists know that some sharks have a sense of taste, they're not sure if the hammerhead shark does.

A hammerhead's sharp senses are crucial for searching out prey.

A Toothy Grin

Many shark species have huge mouths filled with huge teeth. The size and shape of a hammerhead's mouth and teeth depend on its size and its diet.

Larger hammerheads usually have big, sharp teeth. They are shaped like triangles and have serrated edges. This means they are zigzagged. This design is good for tearing food apart. Smaller hammerheads have flatter teeth. All hammerheads swallow their food whole without chewing.

Like all sharks, the hammerhead constantly loses and regrows its teeth. When one tooth breaks or wears down, it falls out. A new one soon replaces it. Over the course of its life, a single hammerhead shark can go through thousands of teeth.

A hammerhead's sharp teeth make quick work of many different types of prey.

Special Senses

Hammerheads have two unusual senses that help them survive in their ocean home. One is provided by body parts called ampullae of Lorenzini. These are cells found under the hammerhead's skin all over its cephalofoil. Each one is connected by a tiny tube to an opening on the surface of the hammerhead's skin. All living creatures give off electrical signals. The ampullae can sense these signals. As the hammerhead swims, the electrical signals help it find hidden prey. Scientists believe this sense can only work when prey is a couple of feet away.

The hammerhead's other unusual sense comes from body parts called lateral lines. These are special tubes that run under the skin along the hammerhead's sides and in its head. There are cells called neuromasts inside the lateral lines. Neuromasts are like tiny hairs. If another animal swims nearby, vibrations travel through the water. The neuromasts feel the vibrations and tell the shark that the creature is close.

A hammerhead's lateral lines run the length of its body.

Migration and Navigation

Some hammerheads stay in one place all year. Others **migrate** to cooler waters in the summer months. When winter comes, they return to warmer seas. Many hammerhead sharks migrate hundreds of miles each year.

Hammerheads often seem to travel along the same route every year. How do they find their way? Scientists are not sure. One group of scientists thinks the hammerheads might be following a path of magnetic fields on the ocean floor. Earth's crust is covered with weak and strong magnetic areas. The hammerheads might use their ampullae of Lorenzini to find these areas and read them like a map.

Hammerheads might use these navigation skills to travel short distances, too. Some scientists believe that hammerheads pick a safe spot to rest with other hammerheads and return to this same location every day. This is called **refuging**.

Scalloped hammerheads can be found returning to the same place each day, forming large groups there.

Always in Motion

Many scientists believe that the hammerhead shark must never stop moving. There are many reasons why this might be true. One is that the hammerhead might sink if it isn't constantly swimming. Most fish have an air **bladder** that keeps them afloat, but sharks do not. Instead, a shark has a liver that is filled with oil. This oil is lighter than water. It helps the shark float, but there are sharks that need extra assistance. The hammerhead also stays on the move to help its blood **circulate**. Sharks have very low blood pressure. Blood could not move around a hammerhead's body if the shark stayed still.

    Hammerheads use a method of breathing called ram ventilation. As a hammerhead swims forward, water comes through its mouth and over its gills. The gills then pull oxygen from the water. Because hammerheads must stay moving to help them breathe, scientists are unsure if these sharks ever sleep. However, there are researchers who believe that hammerheads can sleep while continuing to swim.

A hammerhead's gills are located just behind its head.

CHAPTER 3

Social Life

Hammerheads are among the few types of sharks that come together in a group. A group of hammerheads is called a school. Members of a school stay together only during the day. When night comes and it is time to hunt for food, hammerheads prefer to be alone.

Only the smaller kinds of hammerheads come together to form schools. Sometimes hundreds of them meet at one time. Scientists have found many areas around the world where large schools of hammerheads come together year after year. They have different ideas about why such massive groups of hammerheads gather. One theory is that the hammerheads want to protect themselves against larger sharks. Another belief is that hammerheads are social and just like to be with other hammerheads. A third reason is that they come together to **mate**.

Scientists are not completely sure why hammerheads sometimes come together to form massive schools.

Time to Mate

Most hammerheads in a school are female. Some are young, and some are older. The older female hammerheads are usually larger and stronger. They push the smaller females out of the way. Then the biggest and strongest females move to the middle of the school. They throw their heads wildly back and forth.

This body language sends a message to the male hammerheads. It tells them the female is interested in mating. The males look for large females to mate with. The number of babies in a female's **litter** depends on her size. The larger the female, the more babies she will have. Small females will only have 2 babies in a litter. The largest species might have more than 40.

The male signals that he wants to mate by biting the female. Hammerheads usually mate near the surface of the water. Other kinds of sharks tend to go to deeper water to mate.

Female hammerheads living in schools compete for dominance within the group and the chance to mate.

Hammerhead Babies

After a male and female hammerhead mate, embryos develop inside the mother. The growing embryos get their food from the mother's body. There are two ways that the mother hammerhead feeds its baby. A milky fluid comes from her uterus and washes over the embryo. The embryo is also attached to the mother by a placenta. Nutrition passes from the mother's body to the developing hammerhead through this special tube. It takes between 8 and 16 months for the baby sharks to develop and be born.

Hammerheads usually give birth in the spring or summer. Many newborn animals are helpless. They depend on their parents for food and protection. However, there are no family relationships in the world of sharks. As soon as a hammerhead is born, it is ready to feed itself and to live on its own. The baby shark has teeth and knows how to hunt.

FUN FACT! Even though sharks are fish, their embryos develop inside the mother like in most mammals.

Scientists study scalloped hammerhead pups at the Hawaii Institute of Marine Biology to learn more about the species and how it grows.

CHAPTER 4

Family Ties

Sharks have been around for hundreds of millions of years. They were alive even before the dinosaurs roamed the earth. Sharks belong to the fish family. This family split into two groups about 400 million years ago. Those with bones are part of the Osteichthyes group. Those with cartilage skeletons, such as sharks, are part of the Chondrichthyes.

Paleontologists learn about most ancient animals by looking at **fossil** remains. They have found fossils of shark teeth and the spines from their fins, but there are no complete skeletons. Skeletons made of cartilage **disintegrate** after an animal dies. Scientists believe that sharks have not changed very much over time, but they can't know for sure.

The largest prehistoric shark was probably the megalodon. This shark was likely between 43 and 82 feet (13 and 25 m) long. It probably weighed about 50 tons (45 metric tons). This is several times larger than today's great hammerhead shark.

Teeth are the most common megalodon fossils found.

The Shark Family Today

Today, there are more than 450 species of sharks. They vary widely in size, color, and shape. The sawshark is another shark that is named after a tool. Its long, skinny snout is edged with sharp teeth. The frill shark's long body makes it look like an eel. It has 300 sharp, forked teeth that it buries deep into its prey.

The biggest shark is the whale shark. It can be up to 60 feet (18 m) long and weigh up to 45 tons (41 metric tons). The smallest shark is the spined pygmy. It's only about 6 inches (15 cm) long. That is about the length of a pencil.

Some sharks give birth to live offspring, like the hammerhead does. Other species lay eggs. Some sharks combine these two methods. The shark embryo develops in an egg while inside its mother but hatches before it is born.

The teeth along a sawshark's snout alternate between being long and short.

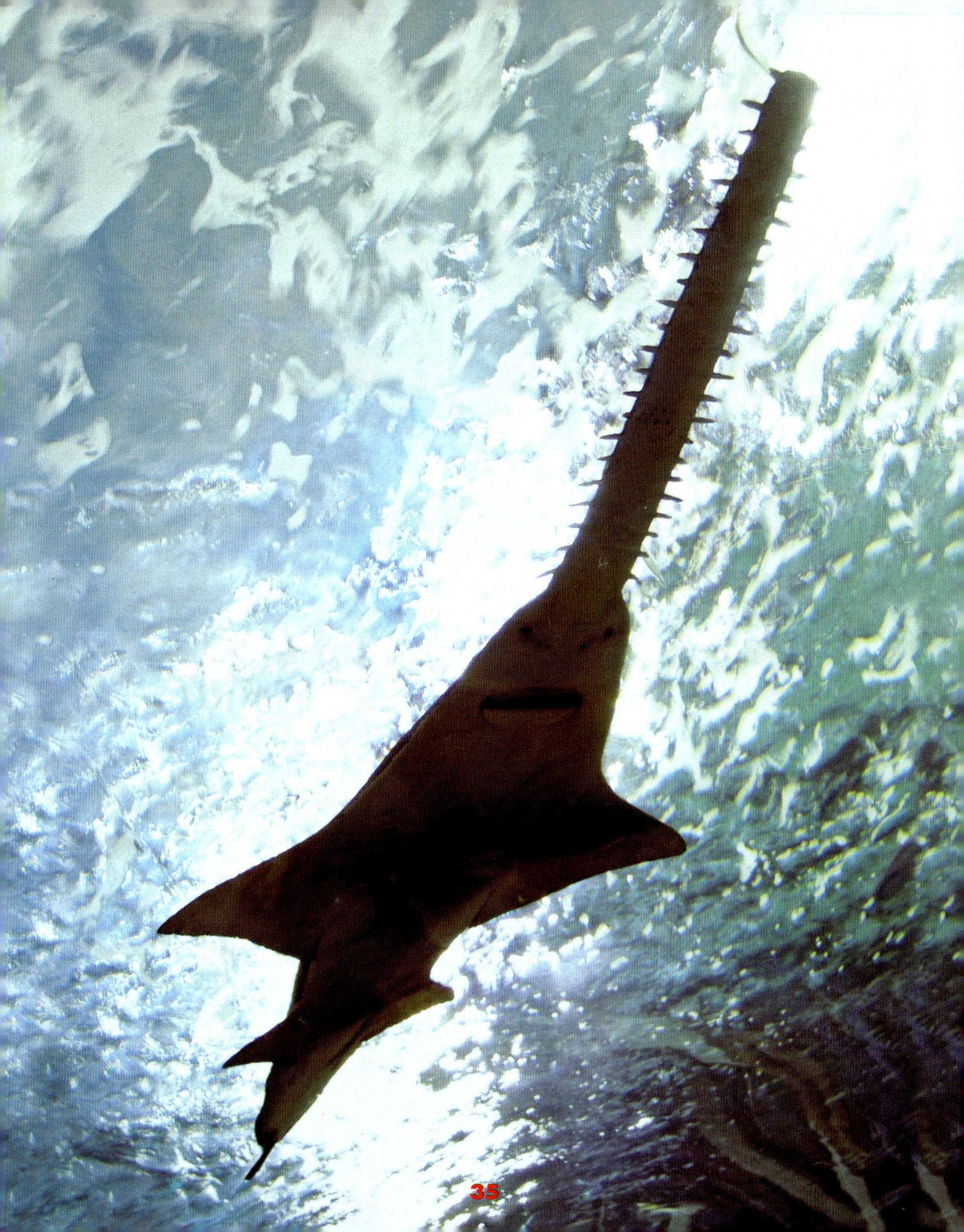

MUNICIPALITY OF ROCKDALE
DANGER
SHARKS IN BOTANY BAY
DOGS ATTRACT SHARKS
PLEASE KEEP
DOGS OUT OF WATER

Not So Scary

Many people find sharks frightening. This isn't too surprising. Sharks can be very large, and they have very sharp teeth. But while they have sometimes been known to attack humans, it doesn't happen very often. On average, there are only around 100 shark attacks each year. Compared to many other risks, the danger of a shark attack is quite small.

However, anyone who spends time in the ocean should still be careful. Sharks are very good at seeing bright colors. Some experts recommend wearing dark colors in the water. It's also a good idea not to wear any sort of metal or jewelry. These can shine like fish scales and make a shark think that a person is something good to eat. A person who has an open wound might want to consider spending the day on the shore. Sharks can detect even the smallest amount of blood in the water.

Some beaches post warning signs that sharks may be nearby, for the safety of both the human visitors and the sharks.

CHAPTER 5

Hard Times for Hammerheads

More than 100 million sharks are killed every year. Almost one-third of all shark species are in danger of **extinction**. Both the great hammerhead and the scalloped hammerhead are considered **endangered**. This means that they are at risk of becoming extinct in the wild.

Many sharks are killed because some people eat shark fin soup. This soup can sell for more than $100 a bowl. Fishers often catch a shark, cut off its fins, and throw the shark back into the ocean to die. The fins are the most valuable part and take up very little room in a fishing boat. This method also enables the fishers to hide the number of sharks they have killed.

In many countries, people believe that shark teeth or other body parts will improve their health or make them more beautiful. Some people like to hunt hammerheads for sport. Other hammerheads die when they are trapped in fishing nets that are put out to catch other marine life.

A hammerhead can drown if it becomes tangled in fishing net.

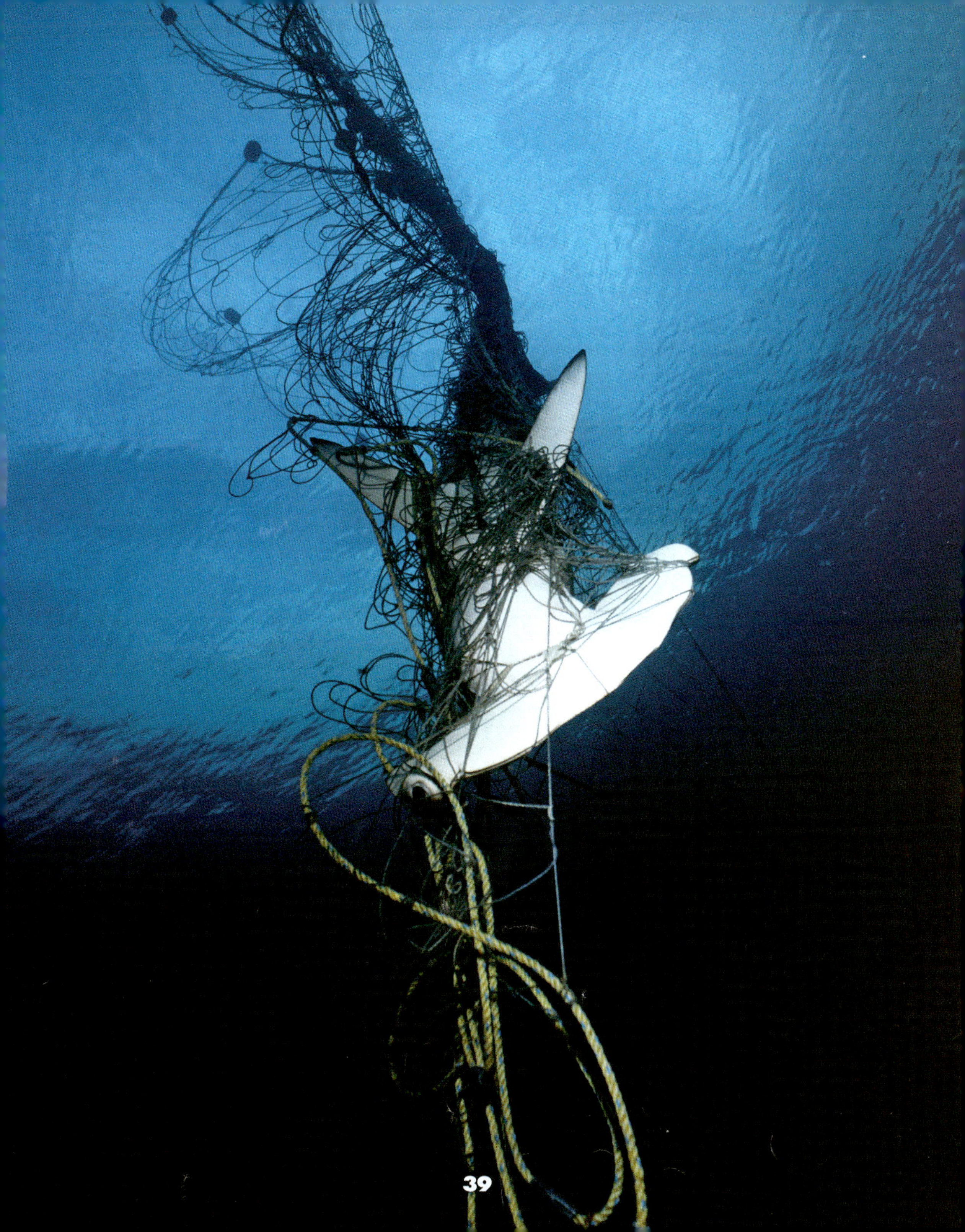

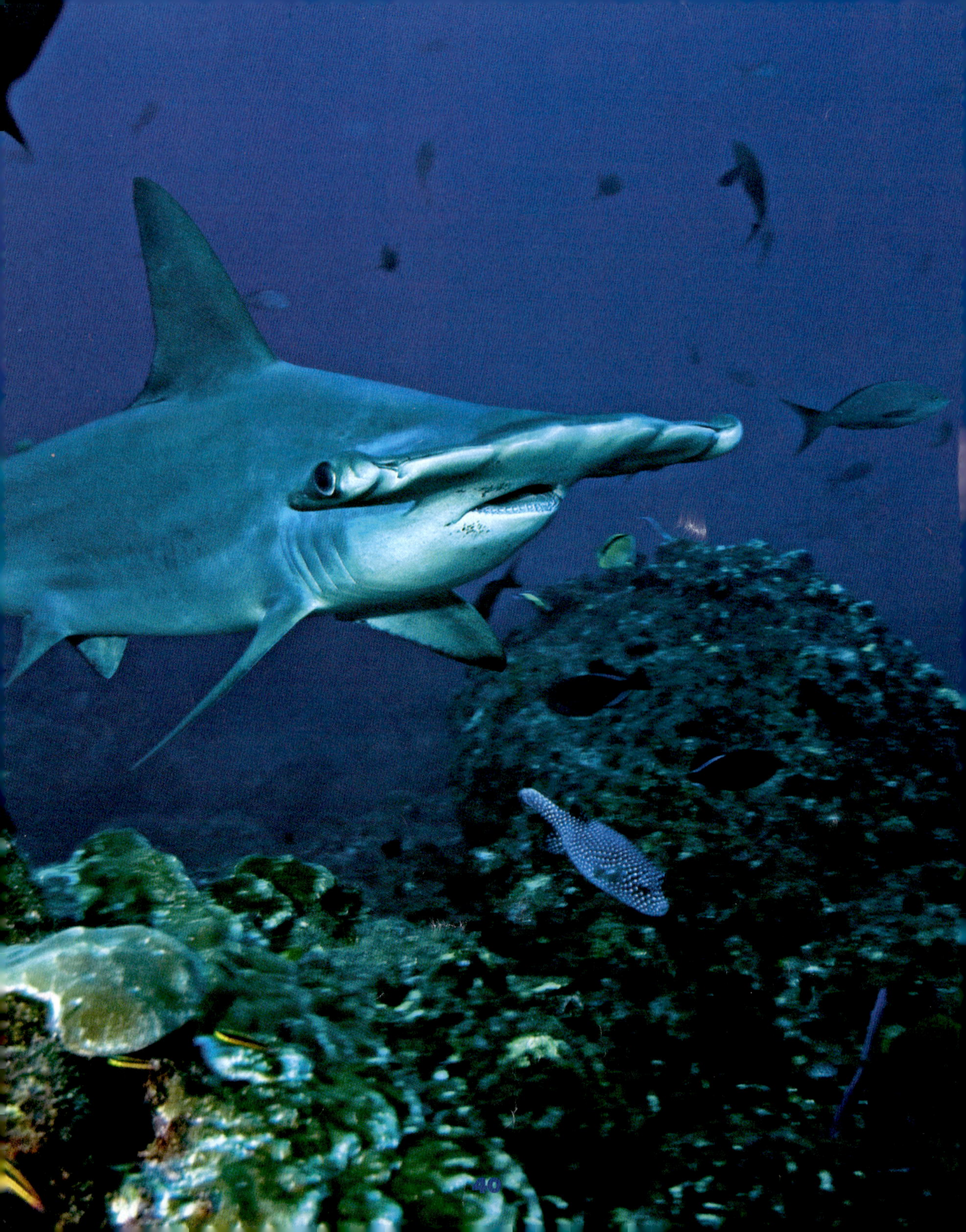

Safer Seas

Unfortunately, most people don't understand how valuable sharks are. They think sharks are scary and don't know that it's important to protect them. However, hammerheads are important to the health of the sea. They control the number of smaller sea creatures in the ocean. If populations of these smaller creatures were allowed to grow too large, they could eat too many underwater plants and destroy coral reefs.

Many countries have tried to help sharks by passing laws about how many can be hunted or sold, but many countries have not done this. Often times the countries that sell the shark fins and body parts are very poor. Shark fishing is a way for their people to make money. Even countries that pass laws to protect sharks aren't always good about following them.

In 2013, people from 170 countries met in Bangkok, Thailand, to talk about ways to protect sharks, including hammerheads. Now is the time for people around the world to work together to protect these important creatures.

With proper education about the roles that hammerheads play in ocean ecosystems, more people will come to respect these incredible creatures instead of fearing them.

Words to Know

bladder (BLAD-ur) — a bag-shaped organ inside the body

carnivores (KAHR-nuh-vorz) — animals that eat meat

cartilage (KAHR-tuh-lij) — a strong, elastic tissue that forms the outer ear and nose of humans and mammals, and lines the bones at the joints

circulate (SUR-kyuh-late) — to move in a circle or pattern

disintegrate (dis-IN-tuh-grate) — to break into small pieces

embryos (EM-bree-ohz) — babies, animals, or plants in the very early stages of development before birth

endangered (en-DAYN-jurd) — at risk of becoming extinct, usually because of human activity

extinction (ik-STINGKT-shuhn) — complete disappearance of a species from a certain area or from the entire world

fossil (FAH-suhl) — a bone, shell, or other trace of an animal or plant from thousands or millions of years ago, preserved as rock

gills (GILZ) — organs that remove oxygen from water to help fish and other underwater animals breathe

litter (LIT-ur) — a number of baby animals that are born at the same time to the same mother

mate (MATE) — to join together to produce babies

migrate (MYE-grate) — to move to another area or climate at a particular time of year

paleontologists (pay-lee-uhn-TAH-luh-jists) — scientists who study fossils and other ancient life-forms

placenta (pluh-SEN-tuh) — the organ that connects a mother to an embryo and is used to deliver food

predators (PRED-uh-turz) — animals that live by hunting other animals for food

prey (PRAY) — an animal that's hunted by another animal for food

refuging (REF-yoo-jing) — finding a safe place to stay

serrated (SER-ay-tid) — having a blade like that of a saw

species (SPEE-sheez) — one of the groups into which animals and plants of the same genus are divided; members of the same species can mate and have offspring

uterus (YOO-tur-uhs) — the hollow organ inside some female animals that holds and nourishes developing offspring

Habitat Map

NORTH AMERICA

SOUTH AMERICA

PACIFIC OCEAN

ATLANTIC

▮ Hammerhead Shark Range

ARCTIC OCEAN

EUROPE

ASIA

AFRICA

PACIFIC OCEAN

OCEAN

INDIAN OCEAN

AUSTRALIA

Find Out More

Books

Green, Sara. *The Hammerhead Shark*. Minneapolis: Bellwether Media, 2013.

Musgrave, Ruth A. *National Geographic Kids Everything Sharks*. Washington DC: National Geographic, 2011.

Randolph, Joanne. *The Hammerhead Shark: Coastal Killer*. New York: PowerKids Press, 2007.

Visit this Scholastic Web site for more information on hammerhead sharks:
www.factsfornow.scholastic.com
Enter the keywords **Hammerhead Sharks**

Index

Page numbers in *italics* indicate a photograph or map.

ampullae of Lorenzini, 21, 22
ancient species, 33

babies. *See* pups.
beaches, *36*
births, 30, 34
blood pressure, 25
body language, 29
body temperature, 9
bonnethead sharks, 10, *10*, *11*, 14
breathing, 17, *24*, 25

Carolina hammerheads, 10
cartilage, 13, 33
caudal fins, 13
cephalofoils, 14, 17, 21
chewing, 18
Chondrichthyes group, 33
colors, *8*, 9, 34, 37
communication, 29
conservation, 41

defenses, 14
denticles, 9
dorsal fins, 13

eggs, 34
embryos, 30, 34
endangered species, 38
extinction, 38
eyes, 6, 14, 37

females, 10, *28*, 29, 30
fins, 6, 13, 33, 38, 41
fishing industry, 38, *39*, 41
food. *See* prey.
fossils, *32*, 33
frill sharks, 34

gills, 17, *24*, 25
great hammerheads, 10, *19*, 33, 38
groups. *See* schools.

habitats, 9, *15*, *40*
Hawaii Institute of Marine Biology, *31*
heads, 6, 14, *15*, 21
hearing, 17
hunting, 6, *12*, *16*, 17, 21, 26, 30, 38, 41

lateral lines, *20*, 21
lengths, 10, *10*, 33, 34
litters, 29
livers, 25

magnetic fields, 22
males, 10, 29
mating, 26, *28*, 29, 30
megalodons, *32*, 33
migration, 22

name origins, 14, 34
navigation, 22
neuromasts, 21

(Index continued)

nostrils, 17

Osteichthyes group, 33

pectoral fins, 13
people, *36*, 37, 38, 41
placentas, 30
predators, 14, 26, 38, 41
prey, 6, 10, 17, 18, *19*, 21, 26, 30, 34, 41
pups, 29, 30, *31*, 34

ram ventilation, 25
refuging, 22, *23*

sawsharks, 34, *35*
scalloped bonnethead sharks, 10
scalloped hammerheads, *7*, 10, *23*, *27*, *31*, 38
schools, 6, *7*, *23*, 26, *27*, *28*, 29

scoophead sharks, 10
senses, 14, *16*, 17, *20*, 21, 22, 37
shapes, 14, *15*, 18, 34
sizes, 10, *10*, 18, 26, 29, 33, 34
skeletons, *12*, 13, 33
smalleye hammerheads, 10
smooth hammerheads, 10
species, 10, 14, *15*, 18, 29, 34, 38
spined pygmy sharks, 34
stingrays, 6, 10
swimming, 6, *11*, 13, 21, 22, *24*, 25

teeth, 18, *19*, 30, *32*, 33, 34, *35*, 37, 38

weight, 10, 33, 34
whale sharks, 34
whitefin hammerheads, 10
winghead sharks, 10

About the Author

Vicky Franchino admits that sharks are not her favorite animal. She saw the movie *Jaws* at an early age—ask your parents about that—and has never quite gotten over it. Franchino does have a good friend named Henry who loves sharks, and she would like to dedicate this book to him. Franchino enjoys learning about new animals and lives in Madison, Wisconsin, with her husband and daughters.

Photo by Kat Franchino

48